OCTAVIO PAZ

ONE WORD TO THE OTHER

ONE WORD TO THE OTHER

Translated by Amelia Simpson

PREFACE

by Julio Ortega

INTRODUCTION

by Juan Hernández-Senter

AFTERWORD

by Eliot Weinberger

One Word To The Other

Natalia d' Arbeloff

Octavio Paz

Latitudes

One Word To The Other

First Edition Paperback, ISBN 0-941179-15-X.

The Spanish version, "De una palabra a otra," is Copyright © 1985 by Octavio Paz, and published by Editorial Seix Barral, S.A.

The English translation is Copyright © 1992 by Amelia Simpson. An earlier version of this translation appeared in *Vortex: A Critical Review* in 1987, published by Latitudes Press.

The Afterword by Eliot Weinberger is Copyright © 1986 by Eliot Weinberger; it is excerpted from his *Works on Paper*, published by New Directions.

The Preface by Julio Ortega appears here in English for the first time, and is Copyright © 1992 by Julio Ortega.

The Introduction by Juan Hernández-Senter was written especially for this edition, and is Copyright © 1992 by Juan Hernández-Senter.

These texts may not be reproduced in any form, except in the case of a review, without written permission from the publisher, Latitudes Press.

The cover art by Mary Clay-Hernández and the art pieces inside the book by Natalia d'Arbeloff are published here with the permission of the artists, but may not be reproduced, except in the case of a review, without the written permission of the publisher, Latitudes Press.

LATITUDES PRESS: Since 1966

Publishers: Robert Bonazzi
Elizabeth Griffin-Bonazzi

Latitudes titles are distributed by Bookslinger, Inc., Small Press Distribution, Inc., Texas Circuit, and by Latitudes Press, P.O. Box 613, Mansfield, TX 76063

Octavio Paz

CERTAINTY

If the white light of this lamp
Is real, if the hand that writes
Is real, are the eyes that observe
What is written also real?

From one word to the other
What I say disappears.
I know I am alive
Between two parentheses.

Translated by Amelia Simpson

PREFACE

by Julio Ortega

We Latin American writers owe Octavio Paz part of our literary identity. After graduating from Borges University in practical deconstructions, we found in Paz's writings the measure of a lasting inquiry of wonder, of reconstructions.

Paz's poetry is shaped by the evidence of both wonder and vulnerability. That is, by epiphany and fugacity as central definitions of poetic perception.

He is probably the last major poet to believe in the powers of poetry as a supra-rational way of knowledge. In fact, he believes more: in poetry as ritual and celebration, as the matter itself of what we are made.

Paz represents the high demand for a literature still capable of dealing with larger issues-love, time, truth. He is saying not only seize the instant but also make it speak, give to time your own voice. Language has here the form of questioning that includes us in its rage, lucidity, and beauty. It reveals the human as the intelligence of the senses.

In a way, he has made of each reader a poet. Because to read his poetry is an act of self-revelation: here poetry speaks for yourself.

As profoundly Latin American, Paz's poetry is rooted in the community of languages, the rituals of belief, the history of plurality, and the search for a tribal as well a modern word of self-affirmation. It is baroque by day and classic by night: it evolves from the hymn to the soliloquy, from song to irony, from lyricism to criticism.

I started reading Octavio Paz in 1961. It has been a long astonishing conversation.

INTRODUCTION

by Juan Hernández-Senter

Octavio Paz states that he wrote his latest book, *Pequeña crónica de grandes días*, "por fidelidad a mí mismo," and that the title of his series of articles is "an echo (and a response)" to another book, one written by Quevedo around 1621. Paz has always tried to be true to himself -- the "other self," the one that "invents," "the friend," "the judge, the victim, the witness," the Paz that "invents himself daily." Furthermore, all of his work has been criticism, translation, an "echo and a response" to other works.

Like *Pequeña crónica de grandes días, One Word To The Other* is also "a short chronicle," not of "grandes días," not of "experiences," but of a life of reading and of "the search for others." Two persons with the name Octavio Paz are presented here. One is the poet, who exists only as "a fiction, a figure of speech." The other person is the "real person," "the first reader," the one who carefully edits and gives the poem its final form. Paz, the editor, says he follows the example of Wordsworth,

Mallarmé, Yeats, Jiménez and Borges. Revising the "spontaneity or dream" is justifiable if one is faithful to the poet and to the poem, he says. The "real person," not the poet, is capable of balancing fiction and reality. If in *Libertad bajo palabra*, a collection of some of his earliest poems, the poet-creator role is stressed, ("Avanzo lentamente y pueblo la noche de estrellas, de palabras"), in *One Word To The Other* greater emphasis is placed on the poem: "what counts isn't the poet but the poem" and "true art demands the sacrifice of the real person in favor of the living mask."

In *Renga*, a poem collectively written by Paz and three other poets (and in four languages), this prominence of the poem over the poet is evident. Paz says in the introduction that "the practice of the renga implies the negation of certain cardinal western notions, such as the belief in the soul and in the reality of the I." In a previous work, *Corriente alterna* an emphasis on the internal reality of the poem had been presented. To understand a poem one should not look to the poet but "rather inside the poem . . . [to] what the words have to say to each other." Persisting on the importance of the poem over authorship, Paz says in *One Word To The Other* that in his writings he is only "reproducing other ghosts." As Paz "the first reader" examines the poetry of last year's Nobel Prize Winner for Literature, he recognizes many ghosts: the many ghosts of the self and the many ghosts that have influenced his writing. True to the poet, the critic, the translator, and to the ghosts in his poetry, Paz presents here a biography of his readings, a "poetic biography . . . made of the confessions of many strangers."

ONE WORD TO THE OTHER

To Pere Gimferrer

Octavio Paz

I was invited to give a public reading of a few selections from my published book *Poems 1935-1975* (Seix Barral, 1978) in Mexico City (August 1979). There were three readings with commentaries. I reproduce here the comments to the first reading, revised and expanded.

ONE WORD TO THE OTHER

In my youth there was a lot of talk about "the poetic experience." I never completely understood what was meant by this expression. Experiences aren't "poetic." Neither are they really "experiences": they're acts, sensations, thoughts--life. Only afterwards, culled by memory and reflection, do those moments become experiences. But that which we see through the eyes of memory isn't the same as that which we live: life is irrecoverable. Poetry is not life, it's the transfiguration of life. It's not living but saying.

These pages are not about my experiences. They aren't memoirs: they're a poetic itinerary. I speak of works I read but I refer almost exclusively to poets and poems; I barely allude to novels, travel books or works of philosophy, history, anthropology, although they have been no less decisive in my formation than the poems I've read. Neither do I speak of countries, cities, houses, landscapes, monuments, illnesses, encounters, friendships and enemies, love affairs, beliefs, changes of fortune and of ideas--everything that's been my life and the reason for my writing.

Is it possible to separate a work of art from life? Goethe once said that poetry is born of circumstance. I think he was right. At least in my case: everything I've written has been a product of circumstance, a response to exterior and interior stimuli.

The monologue of the poet is always a dialogue with the world or with the self. As such, my poems are a kind of emotional, sentimental and spiritual biography. Nevertheless, on gathering these poems I've written over fifty years in one book, I realize that it deals with the biography of a ghost. To put it a better way, of many ghosts. The poems I will read tonight, written forty or twenty-five years ago, did I really write them? Am I the same? This book has been written by a succession of poets: all have vanished and all that remains of them are their words. My poetic biography is made of the confessions of many strangers. We walk always among specters.

Knowing that I'm not the one who has written my poems, I've taken the liberty of revising them. Have I committed any abuse, have I usurped the voice of someone who has disappeared? The truth is that I followed the example of certain poets I admire: Wordsworth, Mallarmé, Yeats. In the Spanish language Juan Ramón Jiménez and Jorge Luis Borges also have revised their writing from time to time. This practice is justifiable for one reason: what counts isn't the poet but the poem. Once, without realizing I was writing a terrible truth I said: the poem exists at the expense of the poet.

The poet who writes the poem isn't the same as the person who goes by that name. The real person--no matter how fugitive his reality--possesses a physical, social and psychic consistency; he has a body and a face, he responds to his name, he was born in Mexico or in Culiacán, his parents are called Pedro and Julia, his sister is Maria, his friend is Alberto, he's dark and thin, he likes the color blue, he plays baseball and goes to Mass but never confesses or takes Communion. On the other hand, the poet isn't a real person: he is a fiction, a figure of speech.

Between the more or less real person and the figure of the poet relations are at once innocent and circumspect. If the poet's fiction devours the real person, what's left is a character: the mask devours the face. If the real person is superimposed on the poet, the mask evaporates and with it the poem itself, which isn't a work of art any longer but is converted into a document. This is what has happened with much modern poetry. All my life I have struggled against this error: the poem is neither confession nor document. To write poems is to balance, like a tightrope walker on a loose rope, between the fiction and the reality, the mask and the face. The poet must sacrifice his real face in order to make his mask more alive and believable: at the same time he must take care that his mask is not immobilized but rather that it have the mobility--and more: the vivacity--of his face. Eliot said that poetry is impersonal. Without doubt, he meant that true art demands the sacrifice of the real person in favor of the living mask. I reworked my poems because I wanted to be faithful to the poet who wrote them, not to the person I was. Faithful to the author of a few poems of which I, the real person, was nothing more than their first reader. I didn't try to change ideas, emotions and sentiments but rather to improve the expression of those sentiments, ideas and emotions. I tried to respect the poet who wrote those poems and not touch that which is called, inexactly, the content; I only tried to speak with greater economy and simplicity. My changes were meant only as purifications. And purity means sacrifice: I obeyed a desire for perfection. Naturally, it's possible that I've made a mistake more than a few times. To write is a risk and to revise what's been written is a greater risk.

◑

I began to write when I was a child. But I only became conscious of what I was doing in adolescence. I belong to a generation initiated at a time when everywhere the great revolution in the arts that we label with an unpleasant military term was declining: the avant-garde. The avant-garde began in Europe around 1910; around 1935 the era of adventure and experimentation appears to come to a close. The last protagonists of the poetic avant-garde in the Spanish language--the Generation of '27 in Spain and that of the Contemporaries in Mexico, return to order. Some, to fixed, traditional forms: sonnets, decimas, romances, tercets; others, to free but not experimental forms, such as Neruda's social poems. The exceptions were Vallejo and Huidobro. As young writers, then, we began to write at a time of a general return to tradition. Ten or fifteen years later, we rediscovered the avant-garde. In contrast to that of 1920, ours didn't have manifestos or groups. It was an avant-garde of solitary, or, more precisely, isolated poets.

In my adolescence I admired above all those poets infused with a solar joy, like Carlos Pellicer, Gerardo Diego, Rafael Alberti. Later I had more demanding masters like Jorge Guillén, or those possessed by tragic truthfulness, like Luis Cernuda. The generation before mine had rediscovered Spanish baroque poetry. At the beginning we mined that vein. But I read with passion not only Góngora and Quevedo but Lope de Vega, San Juan de la Cruz. Sor Juana and the medieval poets too. Also the great Spanish American modernists: Darío, Lugones and their immediate successors, Juan Ramón Jiménez and, in Mexico, the intense López Velarde.

I wrote sonnets and tercets. It was an attempt to assimilate, simultaneously, traditional poetry--especially that of the seventeenth century-- and contemporary poetry. For example, in one of my sonnets, the first line, because of its rhythm and syntax, is a sort of replica of one by Lope de Vega, written in memory of his dead wife. Lope says: "Resuelta en polvo va más siempre hermosa..." And the first line of my sonnet: "Inmóvil en la luz, pero danzante..." I soon abandoned the neo-baroque aesthetic of the previous generation and attempted to create a more direct poetry. I meant to respect perceived reality; without falling into descriptive poetry, I affirmed the existence of the external world. Visual and tactile reality have always been a source of wonder to me. I shifted, too, from long meters--eleven and fourteen syllables--to the shorter lines of popular forms. I learned a lot from medieval poetry and from the songs and traditional forms of the sixteenth and seventeenth centuries. From reading those, I arrived at what Henríquez Ureña has called "irregular versification," that is to say, at accented versification, which is the basis of free verse in Spanish.

Around 1944 another shift occurred in my poetry. As so many other modern poets had done before and as so many would do later, I discovered the language of conversation, colloquial language. Not that of popular traditional poetry--like the poems of a previous period--but rather the language of the city. That language isn't really prose, as has been said, but spoken language. True prose isn't spoken: it's written. Modern poetry tends to be attached to writing but now and then, in a cyclical manner, it rediscovers spoken language. In this way it's reanimated, it returns to its origin: poetry is, primordially, the rhythmic word we hear; only later is it a design we read on paper.

English and North American poetry were not absent from my discovery of the expressive powers of spoken language. I spent some time (1944 and 1945) in San Francisco and in New York. I read with fervor the North American poets, especially T.S. Eliot. Among the English, I was captivated by Yeats whom I continue to read. A double revelation: Blake and Coleridge. They couldn't be more different and perhaps because of that they fascinate me: something leads me to embrace opposites. Reading the Spanish seventeenth century poets prepared me for Donne--since then I have returned to him often--and to the other "metaphysicians." I only began to read and love Wordsworth many years later. Finally, and only very recently, have I managed to understand Pope.

The poetry of the city led me to another experience: that of the oneiric. The transition from colloquialism to the oneiric can be seen by comparing two poems written in 1945: "Elegía interrumpida" and "Virgen." This second one, alludes, of course, to the Christian virgin but also to Diana, the goddess of hunting; and, at the same time, to the modern woman or, at least, a certain type of modern woman, whose archetype isn't Venus but Diana. The poem, divided into four parts, has the dream logic which is analogous to that of myths. The oneiric was the path to surrealistic poetry. The movement attracted me not only for artistic reasons but also because of the alliance of subversion, eroticism and poetry. These three elements had been disassociated, first with the symbolists and later by the first avant-garde, more concerned with the formal problems of art, as is seen in its two most rigorous and radical expressions: cubism and abstract art. Surrealism united life and poetry once again. It was a return to the origin of modern art: Romanticism.

Surrealism is defined by two words opposite in meaning but close phonetically: rebellion and revelation. Both are romantic words. Moreover, despite their opposition, they've been inseparable since the end of the eighteenth century: rebellion is founded on revelation. From the beginning, surrealistic politics were nourished by a poetic. Revelation is a word full of prophetic, gnostic and --why not admit it?--religious resonances. Occultism was one of the currents of surrealism. I confess I was always skeptical of Breton and his friends' inclinations, although hermeticism, perhaps because of its Platonic origins, always interested me--and more: I still have a passion for it. In any case, after nationalism and posiiivism, surrealism, in the first half of the twentieth century, rediscovered like the Romantics a century before, that other sense with which, in certain moments, we perceive a beyond which is not beyond but right here.

The spiritual dimension of the surrealistic poets has a counterpart: the aesthetic dimension. One of the precepts of the surrealists, inherited from Apollinaire, was to astonish and to experience the marvelous. The aesthetic of the marvelous joins that of surprise and both are resolved in the cult of the image. Since I began to write--it was not in vain that I passionately read Góngora and Quevedo--the image for me had been the central element of the poem. The influence of the previous generation--above and beyond all, Huidobro--was decisive. For my whole generation poetry began as an algebra of metaphors. But surrealism set fire to the algebraic equations. Its concept of language as combustible material conquered me: the flame was my poetic test. Of course, not infrequently those flames were theatrical flames; one of the worst affectations of surrealism was the simulation of delirium. Breton was no great admirer of baroque art; nevertheless, it's not impossible to see an inspiration from mannerism in many surrealist manifestations. As for me: surrealism freed my images and set them loose to fly. I heard my thoughts thinking me when I seemed not to be thinking anything; I set off, with eyes closed, through the marvelous forest: the forest of distraction.

☯

Towards the end of 1945, after two years in the United States, I entered the Mexican Foreign Service. The job was modest but it spared me the anxieties and difficulties that I had experienced up to then. They sent me to Paris and I lived there for a long period. Around the middle of 1951, they transferred me to New Delhi and, after a few months, to Tokyo. My stay in the Orient didn't last long: I returned to Europe and by the end of 1953 I was back in Mexico. It was an absence of nine years. I repeat that cipher with emphasis; it was a real gestation. But a backwards gestation: not inside but outside my native land.

During those years my ideas changed, my friendships, my feelings, my hatreds and loves--but I was faithful to poetry. I read and reread poets like those in love read love letters or the devout repeat a prayer every night to their patron saint. Love and devotion are words that designate very diverse sentiments and sensations: adoration, jealousy, envy, spite, irony, sometimes disillusionment, deception. Like dreams for Nerval, poetry was my second life. Or to put it a better way, it was the mirror of my life. An animated mirror that not only repeated my image but also illuminated and deciphered it, as if each one of my acts were a metaphor--almost always weak, imperfect--of another richer reality. A demanding mirror, often critical; reading one poem or another, I blushed and felt embarrassed for myself. Poetry helped me to penetrate myself intimately and to know myself a little: it was knowledge and self-knowledge.

Why did the ancient philosophers look upon poetic fabulation with such disdain? Perhaps because ancient philosophy, except in the case of the stoics, was never interested in particular truths or in human character. Instead of the spectacle of imperfect and irregular human souls, Plato preferred to contemplate the celestial bodies, which seemed to him reason itself, made light and its numbers visible. True wisdom was in the heavens, the sublunar world was ruled by chance, that is, by the passions. Aristotle had more curiosity for nature's enigmas--for example, gestation--than for psychology. Socrates' "Know thyself" was practiced more by poets than philosophers. Euripides and Terence, Catullus and Propertius told me more about men and women than the great metaphysicians. Poetry not only guided me from within: it also opened me to participation in other destinies and in this way led me to a broader, and simultaneously, more intimate understanding of man. To recognize in the lines of a poem a thought or sensation that I, albeit confusedly, had thought or lived, was a kind of confirmation, in the sacramental sense of the word. Recognition and, at the same time, transfiguration: my thoughts and my acts rhymed, if I may use that expression, with those of the poet. Poetry wasn't just a choice but a fraternity. Without poetry I would never have understood the real meaning of resemblance.

I belong to a Francophile family. When I was about fifteen or sixteen I read Galdós' Episodios Nacionales and Salvador Monsalud immediately became one of my heroes. He still is. Although I read the French poets in my adolescence, surrealism taught me to read them another way. I rediscovered Hugo, disowned by the previous generation, and I understood why Darío had admired him so much. My great passion was and is Nerval: I always read him, his prose as well as his poetry. And Baudelaire? He didn't provoke the "shivers" in me: the perverse themes that scandalized his contemporaries bore me; I'm thrilled, instead, by the harmony of his phrase, united with the vision, between lucid and melancholic, of the gnostic Christian who believes in the ontological reality of evil. Number and anguish, cadence and despair, in profound unity, "vaste comme la nuit et comme la clarté." And the modern ones. I was attracted, again, to the extremes: Apollinaire and Valéry.

Later I would return to poets whom I repudiated under the influence of surrealistic Jansenism: Laforgue, the tight-rope walker who dances on the hanged man's rope, and two masters of the most difficult art, that of the trill resolved in murmur and silence: Verlaine and Toulet. Much later I felt attraction, real idolatry, for Mallarmé. One of my antidotes was Ronsard. These two poets are two universes: the atom and the globe. I read a lot of Rimbaud and wrote about him--a great deal. Did that fervor come from true understanding or was it an act of faith--or rather: a superstition? I wouldn't know what to say now: I feel far from Rimbaud. I think we often read things in his poems that he didn't write. But his *Illuminations,* if they didn't illuminate me, marked not a few pages of *¿Aguila o Sol?*

In those years I also explored the Germanic domain. In my undergraduate years I had read Goethe with respect and Heine with enthusiasm. I read pre-Becquer translations of Eulogio Florentino Sanz and those of Llorente, Herrero and the superior ones of Enrique Díez-Canedo. I was especially impressed by the prose: the brilliant and entertaining Cuadros de Viaje and the response to Madame de Stael's celebrated book. This book was my first exposure to the German Romantics. Heine's biting portraits and opinions didn't make them displeasing; on the contrary, I guessed that, without them, modern poetry wouldn't be what it's been. German poetry and philosophy were sources for Coleridge as well as the French Romantics. Nerval was the first to translate Heine into French. Many of his versions of *L'Intermezzo* and *El Mar del Norte* are equal to his admirable translation of *Faust*; nevertheless, the work of the "bon Gérard si naive et si plate" seemed inferior to a pedantic professor so that he felt obligated, a few years ago, to revise it. Another initiation: reading Schopenhahuer and Nietzsche. These two philosophers prepared me to better understand

Hölderlin and Novalis. To read those poets was like retracing a path and returning to the beginning.

A discovery in my adolescence: Jáuregui's translation of Tasso's *A minta*, found by chance in my grandfather's library. Years later I experienced a shock: Leopardi. Reading him has left a mark on my ideas and my vision of things. During the second stay in Paris (1959-1961) I came back to him and it occurred to me to translate five of his poems. At the same time--again the desire to join extremes--I translated two of Marino's sonnets, one of them dedicated to a black woman ("Nera si, ma se'bella, o di Natura / fra le belle d'Amor leggiadro mostro"). I lost those translations, with other papers and letters, on leaving Paris, in 1962.

At almost the same time that I abandoned myself--though lucidly--to the flow of an interior murmur, I began to read the Japanese poets and later the Chinese. It was an unconscious attempt to build a dam against the surrealist overflow. I was captivated by the economy of form: minimal and precise constructions made from a few syllables capable of containing a universe. Undoubtedly there was an echo in my previous reading of popular Spanish poetry in my love for those poetic forms: for many years one of my bedside books was Dámaso Alonso's *Antología de la Poesía Medieval y Tradicional*. My passion for Chinese and Japanese poetry precedes my first trip to the Orient. It began towards the end of 1945, in New York. My stay in that city coincided with the death of Tablada, who had been living in Manhattan for years. I went to the New York Public Library, asked for his books and reread them. That reading was as stimulating as reading Gómez de la Serna had been years before. Tablada's example led me to explore the literature of Japan, and later China, on my own. Certainly, I think I've contributed a little to the re-evaluation of this unjustly neglected poet. Tablada is called a minor poet but what does that mean? A gram of poetry weighs more than a ton of rhetoric.

My first trip to the Orient gave me the opportunity to deepen and broaden my reading of Chinese and Japanese poetry. On the other hand, India's poetry--in contrast to what happened to me with India's thought, plastic arts and music--didn't touch me. Only years later, when I came to know the vernacular poets and the Bengalese tantric tradition, did Indian poetry win me over. I read a great many translations of Japanese and Chinese poetry ana among them I fondly remember those of Arthur Waley. He's one of my patron saints. On my return to Mexico, encouraged by Donald Keene--another one of my guides--I took the liberty of translating, with Eikichi Hayashiya's help, Basho's haibum: "Oku no Hosomichi." Later on, with Wai Lim-Yip's and other friends' help, using various versions and phonetic transcriptions, I translated some poems by Wang Wei, Tu Fu, Su Tong-p'o and others. Those translations--and all the others I've done--are homages: with them I've tried not so much to pay a debt we contract with each poet who enlightens or enchants us as to raise a fragile monument to their memory. More than poetic exercises, they have been recreations, in the double sense of the word. My opinions about writing--I believe I'm no exception--go from one extreme to the other; sometimes I like what I've written a lot, other times I find it abominable, or, what's sadder, insignificant. But I have an innocent vanity: I like some of my translations.

When I began to write, almost no one, in Mexico, took a serious interest in Precolombian poetry. Alfonso Reyes had cited a large fragment of a poem (or a series of poems?) in the last pages of Visión de Anáhuac: "Ninoyolnonotza." It's a version by José María Vigil of Brinton's English translation, only Padre Garibay points out that Brinton knew very little Nahuatl, and as such made use of a Spanish version: Vigil's version was a translation into Spanish of an English translation of a Spanish translation of a Nahuatl original. Reyes' opinions were intelligent and acute--he was always guided by that sensitivity which, in him, by I don't know what spiritual mechanism, was converted into a sort of second and more cordial intelligence. But those opinions were also condescending: he thought, like almost everyone of his generation, that Indians were primitives. The poets of the generation preceding mine (the Contemporaries) weren't attracted either to the indigenous world, except for Carlos Pellicer. Unfortunately, Pellicer's enthusiasm required only eyes and the sense of touch: he was more sensitive to a monument or a sculpture than to a text which, in order to love, we first must decipher. Bernardo Ortiz de Montellano, a little later, showed a more intelligent and lucid love for indigenous poetry. A pity only Rubén M. Campos' book was available to him: *La Producción Literaria de los Aztecas* (Mexico, 1936), valuable as an antecedent but, as Garibay says, "modest." The latter's translations, followed by those of Miguel León Portilla, changed the picture: a new world appeared before us. Nevertheless, I remember that the publication of Padre Garibay's first anthology (*Poesía Indígena del Altiplano*, Mexico, 1940) was highly criticized by one of my friends. This attitude repeated that of the Europeans and North Americans, who for many years insisted on seeing works of Precolombian art as simple ethnographic documents. When the first exhibition of Mexican art was shown in Paris, in 1951, we couldn't overcome the resistance of the director of the Petit Palais, who refused to offer his museum because the exhibition seemed more ethnographic than artistic to him. A few years later that resistance disappeared; Precolumbian art and poetry won over many writers and poets. Novo's enthusiasm was such that he began--an admirable gesture--to learn Nahuatl.

My fondness for Nahuatl poetry is inseparable from my exploration of modern poetry. Although I avidly read Garibay's first translations, I wasn't prepared, poetically, to understand them. I had to pass through the experience of modern art and thought--I'm thinking not only of surrealist poetry but of anthropology as well--in order to penetrate, dazzled, that labyrinth of form-concepts and idea-images that a poem or a Pre-Cortesian sculpture is.

36

Now, from time to time, I go back to those poems. I must confess: their hermeticism tires me. On the other hand, I marvel, like thirty years ago, at the short, lovely poems and riddles of the Otomies. Like archaic figurines, those poems possess a freshness that can only be called ancient. With the years I'm attracted more to the beginnings and ends of civilizations than to their mature eras. The two great tests of the value of a spirit or a society are knowing how to begin and knowing how to end. But in those years in Paris I read a Nahuatl poem with the same enthusiasm with which I attended a Matta or Max Ernst exhibition. That reading left its mark on *Semillas para un Himno* and on other poems such as *Himno entre Ruinas, El cántaro roto* and *Piedra de Sol*.

In a little volume called *La Estación Violenta* (1958), compiled after *Libertad bajo Palabra*, my poetic evolution reaches an end. It is composed of nine long poems, written between 1948 and 1957 in various places: Paris, Naples, Geneva, Venice, Tokyo, Delhi, Mexico. The title comes from a line by Apollinaire that I would have liked, in another country, to use as a chivalric emblem: "Oh sol, es el tiempo de la razón ardiente." Apollinaire's simultaneity--modified by Eliot and Pound--showed me how to say certain things. But the things I said in *La Estación Violenta* seem to me to be different from those which those great poets had said. And in the same way: although surrealism has been the poetic movement to which I've felt the greatest moral and spiritual affinity, I never believed in automatic writing nor in dictation by the unconscious. I've written a few pages about this in *El arco y la lira*. To sum up, along this trajectory from the neobaroque of the poems of 1935 to *Piedra de Sol* (1957), I tried to keep a distance from my predecessors and my contemporaries.

Poetry of circumstance or in response to circumstances, *Libertad bajo Palabra* is a testimony, in the correct sense of the word. At the same time, it aspires to be something more than a testimony and thus its paradoxical title. Freedom is the existential, vital element, but subject to one condition: that of art, that of poetry. I've never thought that poetry could be born from mere spontaneity or dream; neither is it the child of a lucid consciousness but rather of the struggle--which is also, at times, an embrace--between the two. In my youth I wrote some prose pieces with a double title: "Vigilias, / Diario de un soñado." The opposition between dream and vigil is another way of expressing the duality that, in my understanding, secretly animates any poetic act: the conditional freedom of the work. That freedom is conditional because spontaneity is achieved not outside form but in it and by means of it.

AFTERWORD

by Eliot Weinberger

Paz is generally read as Latin America's great surrealist poet--that is, as an exotic European. Yet he remains inherently Mexican, despite the fact that he has always been a cosmopolitan and never a regionalist or an indigenist. Like the hero of a Sufi parable, Paz traveled abroad to find what was always at home. He discovered synesthesia in Rimbaud's colored vowels, not in the Aztec "painted songs." He practiced dissolving the poet's ego through automatic writing and Japanese renga, but he came from a tradition that did not distinguish between poet and poem, where the poet declared, "God has sent me as a messenger,/I am transformed into a poem."

Mexico--a xenophobe whom strangers won't leave alone--has been the center of a global mandala. It is this configuration that Octavio Paz has, in his life and in the work, traced to its furthest reaches. A great synthesizer, he has transformed the picture while simultaneously drawing his own self-portrait.

Born in a suburb of Mexico City in 1914, Paz began at the center and followed the Mexican mandala in three directions. East: as a young Marxist to the Spanish Civil War, and as a surrealist to Paris in the late 1940s. North: to San Francisco and New York during the Second World War, and in the 1970s to various American universities. West: to India and Japan in 1952, and as the Mexican ambassador to India from 1962 to 1968.

From the U.S. he gained a vision of overdevelopment and a view of his own country on the outskirts of history and the pathos of its nationalistic ardor. From Europe, the belief in poetry as "the secret religion of the modern age"; that the revolution of the word is the revolution of the world, and that both cannot exist without a revolution of the body: life as art, a return to the mythic lost unity of thought and body, man and nature, I and the other. From India, and his studies of Buddhism and Tantrism: the revelation of passion binding the world in illusion, and of passion as the liberator of the world: that in the moment of absolute integration, the world dissolves, "transparency is all that remains."

The surrealist motto--"liberty, love and poetry"--applies in varying degrees to most of the modernists of the first half of the century: women and men dedicated to the imagination, to social revolution, to the transformation of all the arts, to the integration of life and art. It seems incredible that that era has passed, that we have entered an age of specialized arts practitioners. Surely others will come, but at the moment Paz is among the last of the poets who drew their own maps of the world.

NOTES

AMELIA SIMPSON (Translator)

Poet, critic and editor—as well as translator—Amelia Simpson is the author of *Detective Fiction from Latin America*, and the editor of an anthology of Latin American tales of crime and mystery scheduled for Spring 1992; both books are published by Fairleigh Dickinson University Press. Her study of Latin American detective fiction traces the development of the genre from its origins in the nineteenth century to the present.

She has a Ph.D. in Spanish American literature from the University of Texas at Austin. Presently she teaches at the University of Florida, Gainesville. Her critical articles and translations (of García Márquez, Paz and Severo Sarduy) have appeared in various journals, including *Vortex: A Critical Review*. Her poems have been in *Affinities* and other magazines.

JULIO ORTEGA (Preface)

Nearly every Spanish-American writer of consequence, from Paz to Fuentes, from Cortázar to Lezama-Lima, has extolled the critical works of Julio Ortega as not merely a reflection but an essential part of the renaissance in twentieth century Spanish-American letters. His *Poetics of Change* (1984) is the foremost critical model for the new narrative of "El Boom"—placing the work of Borges, Fuentes, Rulfo, García Márquez, Cortázar, Lezama-Lima, Carpentier, Cabrera-Infante and Sarduy in startlingly fresh perspective.

A native of Peru, Ortega is considered the ultimate literary arbiter of that country's greatest writers—in particular, his masterful studies of poet César Vallejo and novelist José María Arguedas. A highly respected poet, novelist and dramatist, he has published a dozen books in Spanish and English. Presently, he teaches at Brown University.

JUAN HERNANDEZ-SENTER (Introduction)

Poet, translator, singer-songwriter, Juan Hernández-Senter has three books and four albums to his credit. His first book of poetry, *Misquotations*, has been praised by Mexican masters Juan José Arreola and Ernesto Flores-Flores. Margo Gutierrez, writing in *Books of the Southwest*, called him "a writer to watch." For Latitudes, he has translated two books of poetry by Ernesto Flores-Flores, including *The Past is a Foreign Country*, due out next spring.

A native of Guanajuato, he is the bicultural offspring of Mexican and North American parentage. He grew up in Fort Worth, Texas, working his way through college as a singer. He earned the Ph.D., in English, from Texas Christian University. Presently, he teaches translation at California State University, Long Beach. He is at work on a Spanish translation of *Black Like Me,* John Howard Griffin's classic journal of racism (Signet/New American Library). Hernández-Senter has a second book of poetry ready for publication in Mexico.

ELIOT WEINBERGER (Afterword)

One of this country's greatest translators of Spanish-American literature, Eliot Weinberger has brought no less than six collections by Octavio Paz into English; the latest and most comprehensive is *The Collected Poems, 1957-1987,* published by New Directions, in 1990. Under the same imprint, he has published translations of Borges' *Seven Nights* and *Exaltation of Light,* the poetry of Homero Aridjis. Weinberger's own poetry has been widely published in journals.

Works on Paper (New Directions), Weinberger's collection of essays, reveals him as a candid social observer and penetrating essayist.

NATALIA d'ARBELOFF (Artist)

Born in Paris, she has lived in London since 1963. She is an artist and bookmaker of international reputation, and the author of three books on design-teaching. Her art, articles and cartoons appear in various magazines, including the delightful philosophical cartoon, "The Augustine Strip," which has been in *Resurgence* magazine since 1985.

Natalia d'Arbeloff's magnificent hand-made books are in the rare book libraries at Harvard, Princeton, Columbia, Boston, Stanford, UCLA, Chicago, and many other universities. She is also represented in the New York Public Library, the National Library of Australia, Biblioteca Nazionale in Rome, the Humanities Research Center at the University of Texas at Austin, as well as collections in Paris, Oxford, London, and the Library of Congress in Washington, D.C.

MARY CLAY-HERNANDEZ (Cover Artist)

Born in Texas, she has a degree in art from Texas Christian University. Another of her series of Mexican doorway pieces was the cover for *Misquotations,* a book of poems by Juan Hernández-Senter, published by Latitudes Press. She lives in Fort Worth with her husband and children.

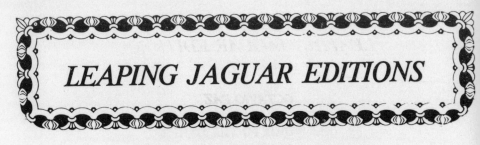

LEAPING JAGUAR EDITIONS

Latin American Texts

Latitudes' series Leaping Jaguar Editions is, without any doubt, one of the best collections of the literature of "El Boom" available in English from any single publisher.

—The Dallas Morning News

Latitudes Press is bringing out what promises to be a wide selection of previously unpublished Latin American texts in translation. Known as Leaping Jaguar Editions, this series has as its first the Selected Writings of Macedonio Fernandez, who was the mentor of Jorge Luis Borges and many others. Called *Macedonio*, this selection of stories, poems and essays includes a portrait of Macedonio by Borges.

—Susan Shafarzek, *Library Journal*

LEAPING JAGUAR EDITIONS

OCTAVIO PAZ

ONE WORD TO THE OTHER
Poetics
Translated by Amelia S. Simpson

MACEDONIO FERNANDEZ

SELECTED WRITINGS
Edited by Jo Anne Englebert
Epilogue by Jorge Luis Borges

JUAN HERNANDEZ-SENTER

MISQUOTATIONS and OTHER POEMS
CITAS EQUIVOCADAS y otros poemas

LOURDES ESPINOLA

WOMANHOOD
and Other Misfortunes
Translated by Naomi Lindstrom

TESSERAE:
A Mosaic of 20th Century Brazilian Poetry
Edited by Charles Richard Carlisle

Latin American Texts
In English, Spanish and Bilingual Editions
(In Print)

LATITUDES PRESS

The critics love it.

One of the finest imprints in the country.

Typically, the journals and books published by Latitudes Press are attractive in design and edited with great care. The affinities offered are those among artists—of various nationalities and techniques—at one in the upward lift of their vision and imagination. Most, if not all, of the writers are also at one in their emphasis—through the rigors of art—on self-discovery. Their direction is "vertical" in a metaphysical sense—grounded in "realism" but "contemporary" and explorative in vision. Latitudes has a healthy balance—or a meeting long overdue—of several Latin American and North American writers who have much in common but who are only now beginning to realize it.

Since 1966

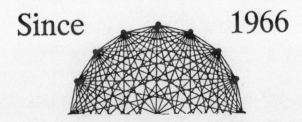

LATITUDES PRESS